I0200576

One Birth, Two Lives.

Pooja Rajendran

BookLeaf
Publishing

India | USA | UK

Made with ❤ on the BookLeaf Publishing Platform
www.bookleafpub.in
www.bookleafpub.com

Dedication

To my mother, who built my roots with unconditional love.
To my teachers at Sacred Heart, who helped me discover my love for the written word.
To my husband, who holds my world together.
And to my son, my reason for being.

Preface

These musings were born in the quiet hours between feeding bottles and unfinished thoughts. With the first breath he took, so did I.

One birth, two lives is an exploration of what it means to be reborn, as a mother, as a woman, as love itself. Through simple moments and quiet truths, these poems hold the ache and the awe, the breaking and the becoming. Reminding us that even in exhaustion, there is grace, and in the ordinary, something divine.

If you find yourself somewhere between those two lines or want a front-row seat to this beautiful, bewildering rollercoaster ride called motherhood, this tiny book of poems is for you.

Acknowledgements

To every mother who lent me a listening ear when I
needed one.
To my friends who reminded me I was still me beyond
the role.
To the readers of this tiny book who chose to pause and
feel these words with me.
To my family, for patience, faith, and love that quietly
carried me here.
And to the divine, who never let me go
and eternally wrapped me with love and care.
Thank you, thank you, thank you.

Lifeline for a lifetime

When one line became two,
The sun felt cool,
The wind danced a duet,
The birds whistled a haiku,
The leaves threw a party in the air,
The clouds forgot to cry,
The sea stood still,
The clocks forgot to cuckoo,
The cats barked,
The dogs meowed,
The moon lost her freckles,
The stars huddled close, conspiring to be a planet,
The mountains let out a century-old sigh,
and time took off its shoes to rest.
As seconds turned to minutes,
and minutes turned to months,
nine, to be exact.
One line became two,
And I found my lifeline for a lifetime in you.

Growing

As motherhood decided to hug me tight,
I felt life growing in me day and night.
My body swayed to a sacred, unseen beat,
What a wonder it is when in your womb, your heart
starts to beat.
The weight I carried gave me a precious gift,
A promise, a blessing to embrace and lift.
I cherished every butterfly flutter and Ronaldo kick,
As a second turned to nine months in a flick.

There's no month like June

February once held the crown.
My birthday, my joy, my sparkle.
But June, oh June, you quietly won.
The day you made me meet my baby son.

The breeze held its breath, the world fell still,
As time made space for infinite love to fill.
The days turned to gold, the nights into rhyme,
The wait had been quiet, the moment divine.

Then you, little wonder, came into view.
You made my whole world brand new.
With eyes full of stars and fingers so small,
You unlocked a love I never knew,
A bond so eternal, gentle, and true.

Now every June, my soul softly sways,
Remembering you and those first sacred days.
For nothing compares, no bloom nor tune.
To the love that I found in the arms of June.

4 am

When 2 became 3,
There's no time for hot tea.
2-minute baths felt like eternity.
Security! Wait, that's me!
Watching, waiting, always on the guard.
Poor Google search, let's bombard.
Baby's poop colour, baby's breathing, baby's latching,
baby's teething.
When mornings and nights are topsy-turvy,
There's always a mix of happiness, pain, delight, and
worry.
But when we drop the load and enjoy the now,
Oh, darling, these 4 am memories are what life is all
about!

Hello from the mother side

Hello, it's me.
Once upon a time, I used to dance till dawn and pass out
on iced tea (the fun kind).

Hello, can you hear me?
My night was day, my day was night,
But it was all for pitches and strategy.

Now, hello from the mother side.
I must have pumped a thousand times.
Tried to catch a wink of sleep,
But all in vain.
My darling Angel is keeping Eastern Standard Time!
So, hello from the mother side.
It's night or day or evening time (who knows anymore?)
All I know is my darling is smiling at me,
Oh, that smile is enough, it's the end of me.

So, hello from the mother side.
I'm enjoying this rollercoaster ride.

Cause I know I'm going to miss this phase,
For the rest of my life.
These moments I'm feeling are what life is about.

So, hello from the mother side.

Behind my shoulder

Who's standing behind my shoulder?
Wee Willie Winkie? Eddie? Shrek?
Who is summoning your keen eye?
A court jester from the medieval era?
An invisible cyborg from the future?
A passing sheep from a dream?
Goldilocks?
Godzilla?
God?
Who is it that you stare deep into?
Is it your great grandma visiting from heaven?
Is it Peeves who has strayed away from the castle?
Or my break dancing spirit animal, or wait, is it your
patronus?
Hey, hey, I'm right here, buddy
But whose eyes are you peering into behind my
shoulder?
Are they your hopes and dreams of tomorrow?
Is it these 4 am memories we are making together?
Whatever it is, my boy, it's come to greet us.

In the wee hours of a cocktail of dusk and dawn on the rocks.

It may be just the two or two hundred of us.

Mama, the true know-it-all

They say a mother is born,
the minute her baby arrives,
But they forget to mention,
Someone else quietly dies.

The woman who once slept through the night,
who rode her scooter with wind in her hair,
who had time to laugh, to cry,
to dream,
to just *be*.

Now she's expected to know it all,
how to soothe, feed, hold, heal,
hunger, aches, weariness ah and how not to feel.
How to smile through pain,
how to love endlessly,
with no one loving her enough
in return.

She learns to rise

from a million emotions
that shoot to the sky and crash all at once
fear, wonder, guilt,
and loneliness
that sinks as low as the seabed.

They say,
"It's just a phase."
But no one stays
to hold her through it.

She gives,
and gives,
until her love fills
every corner of the world
and still,
She stands alone,
the quiet expert of chaos,
the tired know-it-all
called *Mama*.

A mother's mother

I was born twice
once by her hands,
and once again
by the hands that held my child.

She did it for me,
And then she did it all again
every sleepless night,
every trembling prayer,
every ache she once buried
came back,
this time for the life I brought into the world.

When my body broke,
she became my spine.
When my mind drowned,
she carried both me and my baby to shore.

They call it a mother's love,
But I call it

a gift from the divine.

I saw God
not in temples or in miracles,
but in her wrinkled palms,
in her exhausted smile,
in her tired eyes
that still looked only at me,
as her baby held her baby.

If not for her,
No new mother could heal,
No new mother could rise.

And when they call me *Mama*,
I'll remember
She was mine first.

My Two Babies

I have two babies,
one I built with my love for ideas and words,
and one I brought into the world with love.

The first grew out of sleepless nights,
pitch decks and deadlines,
dressed in ideas and ink.

The second came wrapped in cries and warmth,
milk stains and miracles,
a tiny soul who taught me,
What true surrender really means.

I left my first child
in a world that never pauses,
to raise the one who needs my arms.

Will my first wait for me?
Will it remember my touch?
my voice,

the fire that once built it.
Or will it have grown,
moved on,
found someone new to love it back?

Only time can tell.
Some dreams pause,
So bigger ones can come true.

Now, it gives me great pride
to rock this little one to sleep,
whispering to the other
Mama will return.

Today,
This is my full-time role,
to love,
to nurture,
to build,
and then
begin again.

Postpartum Paradox

How can two opposites
coexist so fiercely?

Worry and delight
share a midnight waltz.

Fear and excitement
Take a hike together.

Pain and pleasure
kiss under the moonlight.

Heartbreak and healing
meet quietly by twilight.

A deep slumber
with eyes wide open.
A vertical run
between dusk and dawn.
A smile

that oscillates upside down.

A breathless, breath of fresh air.

So many contradictions,
Yet all of them are true
each one living
within the same tired soul.

Only a mother knows
how joy and ache
can bloom in the same heartbeat,
and still keep beating forevermore.

Hey Stupid

That big can of water I once lifted with ease
Now feels like a mountain in disguise.

Agility took the midnight train.
Stamina eloped with energy.
Flexibility went on a mountain hike,
And peace took a deep-sea dive.

Everything changed.
Oh, how I wish
for the body and mind I had before
So I could mother
with more clarity,
less chaos.

I wear many caps throughout the day,
but a dunce cap seems a permanent part of the set.
What happened to my brain?
The same woman who once juggled ten crises
now stares at one

like an underwater sponge and his starfish buddy
after they dunk their dessert,
completely lost in sweet confusion.

Alas, my brain stays vacant,
Exactly when I need it most.

Maybe this is who I am now,
a softer, slower, sillier version.
Will this new me
ever meet the old?

Relax

When he falls,
my knees hurt.
When he cries,
the tears are mine.
When he frowns,
my heart breaks into pieces
that no one can ever find.

Yet to the world,
It's just a silly mother's worry.

They don't see,
How his fever burns my forehead,
How his bruises tattoo my skin.
"It's just a scratch," they say
But it's a scar on my existence.

Oh, how little they know
whatever my baby feels,
Mama feels it

a thousand times more.

"Oh, silly mama, it's just a kid.
You're just a mother, one among many.
So, relax."

10 Minutes

You stepped out for ten minutes
just ten, I told myself.
You're only going to the park with Dada.

But the walls forgot what to do with silence.
They didn't know how to echo
without your laughter.

The toys waited
mid-sentence, mid-story,
mid-giggle, mid-mess
holding their breath,
waiting for their cue.

The floors grew confused,
Their creaks wandered off without you.

Even the curtains froze mid-sway,
unsure how to move without your pull.

And so, did I
I didn't know how to stand in a room
without a tug on my dress,
without a squeal or a spill,
without someone biting my hand
just to remind me I exist.

It was only ten minutes,
Yet the silence felt like years.
I realized I no longer remember
What the world felt like
before you arrived.

Then the key turned,
and your laughter spilled back in.
The house exhaled,
and so did I.

Save Me a Seat

The life of the party I used to be,
the belle of the ball, everyone's cup of tea.
Sometimes the joker, sometimes the charmer,
Either way, all eyes were on me.

Then motherhood hit like a cannonball
and suddenly, there was no time for me,
leave alone anyone at all.

Now I'm the life of the living room,
the belle of the kitchen,
the joker of the nursery,
the jukebox queen of lullabies.

But friends, do save me a seat.
Maybe one day I'll finally show up to the meet.
Hair unwashed but heart still loud,
ready to toast to the chaos,
ready to steal the crowd.

Thanks but no thanks

"Sleep when the baby sleeps," they so casually say,
Sure, right after I do laundry, cook,
Cry a little and stare at the hallway.

"Have two under two, it's easier!"
Ah, yes, because chaos multiplies into calm.

"Put him in daycare, bounce right back,"
Oh, absolutely, let me just bounce
between guilt, exhaustion, and a smile,
and the illusion of personal choice.

"Don't pick him up too much, let him cry,"
Sure, nothing says strong baby
like a broken lullaby.

"Just wait till he starts walking
That's when the real work begins."
Oh, thank you for rubbing salt in my wounds.
Now, can you please stop barking?

"In our time, we did it all without help."
Congratulations, but I can't be like you.
I stumble, I fumble,
And now and then I yelp.

So, bye-bye when it comes to your advice.
Take it,
wrap it in pretty paper,
tie a bow on it,
and shove it where the sun doesn't shine.
Bye-bye.

Seasons of you

On the day you were born, your eyes were wide open as
you looked at me for the very first time.
I thought I'd have that version of you forever.

In days, I got to see another you as I greeted another me.
Your very first roll over and goofy little grin,
I thought I'd see that version of you forever.

But in a fleeting moment, I saw a whole new you.

You sat up by yourself and smiled at me.
My heart became a mushy puddle.
I thought I'd own that version of you forever.

When your lovely locks began to grow
and I tied them into a tiny fountain head,
I thought I'd have that version of you forever.

You and me in each other's arms at the wee hours of
dusk,

as we walk each other to sleep.
I thought that version of you was mine to keep forever.

The first time you called me mama,
the first peck on the cheek,
the first bite on the hand,
the first everything
I thought they were versions of you that would stay
forever.

Little did I know I couldn't keep these million versions of
you.
They silently came and silently left.

But oh, sweet child,
every version of you
and every version you're going to be
is ctched in my very existence.

Nobody told me

Nobody told me
that I'd feel most alive
when my body is broken,
And so is my spirit.

Nobody told me
that when I need someone the most,
I'd have my own shadow
As I cradle the life I created in my arms.

Nobody told me
that the most peace I'll ever feel
is at 3 a.m. using my last bit of energy
to walk my baby to sleep.

Nobody told me
a house scattered with toys
could clear the clutter in my head.

Nobody told me

about the peace I would find
in the arms of chaos.

Nobody told me
that in losing pieces of myself,
I'd uncover the most beautiful part of me.

The plot twist

What once felt like survival,
transformed into a celebration.

That grip of constant fear
Suddenly loosened its hold,
like a storm,
That wasn't meant to stay.

The everyday routine blossomed
into a ritual.
The mundane became magic.
Exhaustion became excitement.

What a feeling it is
to begin finding myself again,
when the old me and the postpartum me
share one last waltz
before both softly fade,
making room for someone
entirely new. Renewed.

What a joy it is
to celebrate again with colour and laughter,
to feel light enough to dance,
to no longer walk on eggshells of worry,
or break under invisible weight.

The plot twist, after all,
wasn't about becoming who I was,
but realizing who I was always meant to be.

My Son, My Moon, My Star.

My son, my moon, my star so bright,
When I see your smiling face, everything feels right.

The emotions and gratitude I feel for you
They are beyond what I can ever write.

The days are long and sometimes tiring,
But with you, my darling, they are forever bright.

The way you call me *mama,*
the way you gently kiss my cheek,
Seeing you grow makes me so happy,
week after week.

Milk-scented mornings, lullaby nights,
a rhythm only love could write.
Each giggle folds the day into gold,
belly laughs blooming like a jasmine wish in June.
As the morning light dances on your lashes,
I am forever reminded that my wish came true.

My life has never felt this meaningful.
Oh baby, you make mama's heart so full.

With every smile, every kiss,
every version of you,
Amma feels like her whole world
has been made brand new.

You are my every reason, my sweetest delight,
My morning sun and my calmest night.

My Child, My Teacher.

Oh sweet child, how innocent you are.
You see all as one, and one as all.
No race, no border, no fence of belief
Has ever divided your love.

Children love without measure,
they see without judgement,
They embrace without question.

Your heart is unfiltered light,
Your smile knows no side.
Where adults draw lines,
You build bridges.

You remind me that kindness
doesn't need language,
That laughter sounds the same
in every home, every heart.
You teach me that patience
isn't taught but felt,

that joy can live inside
a cardboard box or a simple hi.

You forgive before you're asked to,
You love before you're loved back,
You trust before the world
teaches you to doubt.
And every time I watch your nature unfold,
A part of me is reborn, too
the part that once believed
in pure magic.

Thank you, my child,
for reminding me of who I was
for helping me reach into my own yesterdays
and gather the innocence and faith
I had quietly left behind.

You adapt to every change
with laughter and ease,
while we grown-ups complain
of the smallest breeze.

Oh, to be a child again,
to see the world through wonder,
to love without condition.
I promise I'll learn how to be a better me.

I promise to learn it from you,
my little one.

The I in Village

I chose to do this on my own,
no nanny, no extra hands,
just mine trembling, learning, loving.

No help, who looks at him as work
or a meal ticket,
just a tired heart beating
day in and day out for him,
from the crack of dawn
to the crack of my back.

"Upsy daisy," we whisper,
and begin again,
the same day, the same chaos,
laced with unseen magic.

No village, no casseroles,
no bathroom breaks,
Just me and my love soldiering on.

My mother, my angel, drifts in to help,
a soft bridge between worlds.

Between us, generations merged,
the mother who raised me
helping me raise my child.

Strength isn't found in the crowd,
It's born in the quiet,
in the doing,
in the loving.

I didn't just survive motherhood,
I became it.
And somewhere between his first cry and my quiet sigh,
Two lives were born from one heartbeat,
his, and mine.